CW01512448

*Our thanks are due to Steven Arthur
for his expert advice.*

ISBN 1 85103 080 8

First published 1988 by Editions Gallimard
First published 1990 in Great Britain by Moonlight Publishing Ltd,
36 Stratford Road, London W8
© 1988 Editions Gallimard
English text © 1990 Moonlight Publishing Ltd

Printed in Italy by La Editoriale Libraria

FLYING ACES

DISCOVERERS

Written and illustrated by
James Prunier

Translated by Margaret Malpas

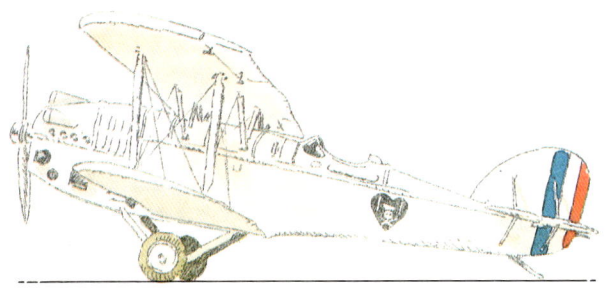

MOONLIGHT PUBLISHING

Contents

Those daring young men ...

By the beginning of the twentieth century, flying was no longer considered a joke. Crowds of people gathered to watch in fascination as aircraft roared over the countryside.

Pilots attempted more daring feats every day. Some even risked flying over big cities, so that the people there could admire the aviators' skilful handling of their strange flying machines.

> *It was miraculous, it was mad! Our dreams then could turn into reality, however daring they might be.*
>
> The architect Le Corbusier, who saw Comte de Lambert's exploit from his window.

One of their most popular stunts, eagerly recorded by the photographers of the time, was to fly round a famous building. In 1909 the Comte de Lambert made a circuit of the Eiffel Tower. Mario Cobianchi flew over the Leaning Tower of Pisa in 1911, and the following year Harry Atwood landed his aircraft on the lawn of the White House in Washington.

Well-known buildings – the bigger the better – were used either as landmarks or as finishing-posts for races and long-distance flights.

Frank McLean flew under Tower Bridge, but moments later his aircraft went out of control and crashed into the Thames.

Technical developments

Development of the cockpit

1908: Santos-Dumont's Demoiselle

1909: Levavasseur's Antoinette

1911: Béchereau's Deperdussin B

1917: Breguet XIV

1910: Igo Etrich's Taube

The years before the First World War saw rapid developments in aircraft construction. Frames were now made of metal instead of wood, though they were still strengthened by wire struts. Plywood was used on the outside of the fuselage, because it was stronger than canvas. The German plane-makers, Dornier and Junkers, even used thin sheet-metal; they chose duralumin, an aluminium alloy which is light but very strong, and stretches without cracking.

Development of ailerons

1908: wing-tip of an Antoinette aircraft

1909: ailerons on Glenn Curtiss's Golden Flyer

Just before 1914, an elegant mono-plane called the Taube ('dove') became the forerunner of generations of fighter planes when large crosses were painted on its wings. Soon, markings of this kind were used on all military aircraft to show which side they were on.

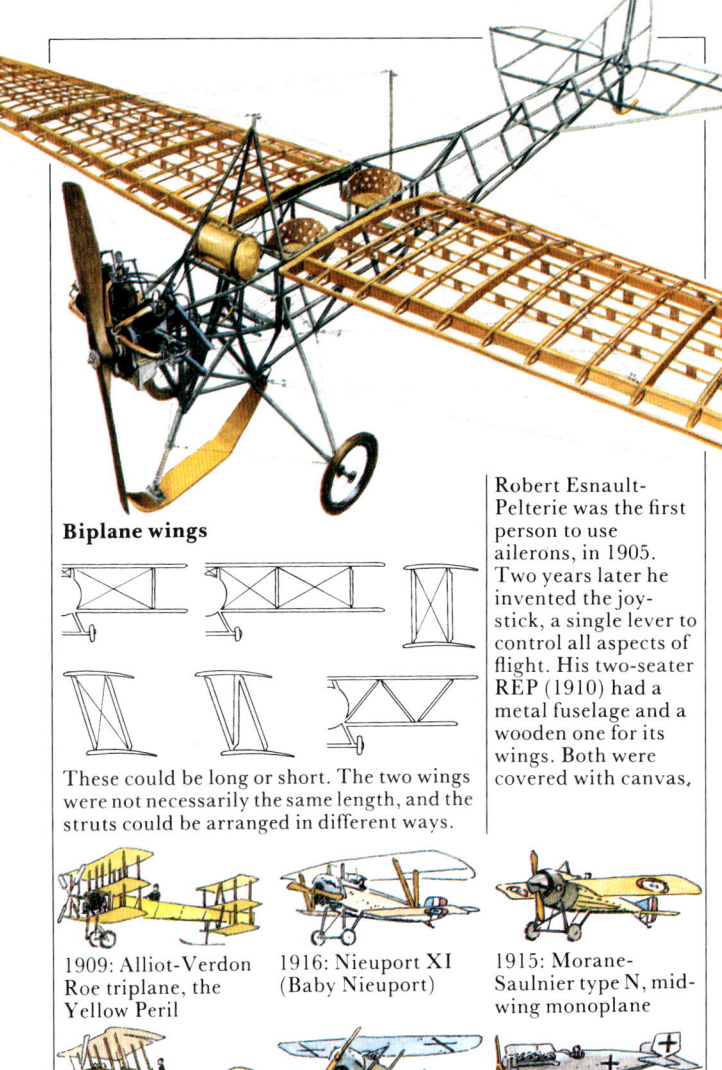

Biplane wings

These could be long or short. The two wings were not necessarily the same length, and the struts could be arranged in different ways.

Robert Esnault-Pelterie was the first person to use ailerons, in 1905. Two years later he invented the joystick, a single lever to control all aspects of flight. His two-seater REP (1910) had a metal fuselage and a wooden one for its wings. Both were covered with canvas,

1909: Alliot-Verdon Roe triplane, the Yellow Peril

1916: Nieuport XI (Baby Nieuport)

1915: Morane-Saulnier type N, mid-wing monoplane

1909: Goupy biplane

1918: Fokker D-VIII monoplane, with umbrella wings

1918: Junkers D-I, low-wing monoplane

Engines and propellers

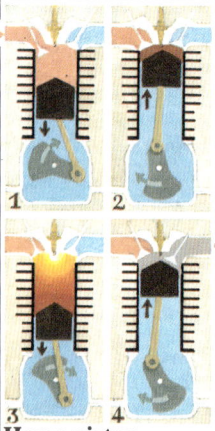

How a piston-engine works

Each piston makes four movements (strokes) during every cycle.
1. Fuel intake: as the piston falls, a mixture of air and fuel is sucked in. The entry valve closes.
2. Compression: the piston rises and compresses the fuel mixture.
3. Ignition: a spark sets light to the fuel, which expands so that the piston is pushed down.
4. Exhaust: the piston rises again and forces the gases out through another valve.

By 1910, most aeroplanes had a cockpit, a pilot's seat inside the fuselage. At this stage, the plane was controlled by one lever and a rudder-bar; there were still hardly any navigational instruments. Eventually, however, the airspeed indicator, the altimeter and the compass appeared in the cockpit, soon followed by all sorts of indicators which showed how the aeroplane was functioning.

The golden age of the piston-engine lasted from 1914 to 1950. There were two main types.

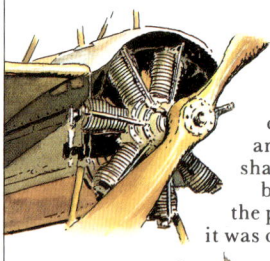

The Gnome rotary engine (1911) had 7 cylinders (50 hp) arranged in a star-shape. The cylinder block turned with the propeller, so that it was cooled by the air.

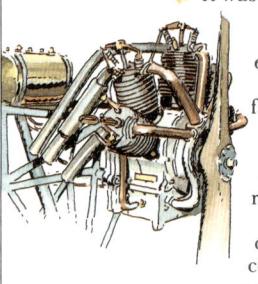

The REP fixed engine (1910) had 5 cylinders in a fan-shape (60 hp). The engine was fixed on the front of the fuselage, at right-angles to the airflow. The cylinders also had cooling-ribs on the outside, to increase the area exposed to the air.

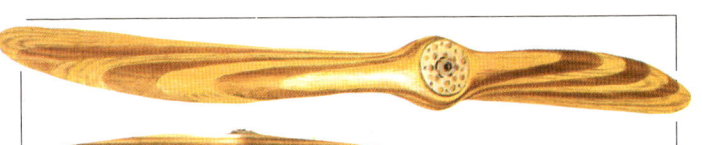

In the first, known as 'in-line' engine, the cylinders lay in a row or in a V-shape, and were cooled by water; in the second, they were arranged in a circle, and were cooled by air. These were generally known as rotary engines.

As the propeller is turned by the engine, it pushes the air round. Unfortunately, this tends to make the plane turn sideways, in the opposite direction to the propeller. The problem, known as torque, can be corrected by altering the angle of either the engine or the tail-fin; another solution is to fit two propellers, turning in opposite directions.

Wooden propeller
Strips of hardwood were glued together, and the whole block was cut to shape. Around 1930, the makers began to use duralumin, which enabled them to make propellers of different shapes.

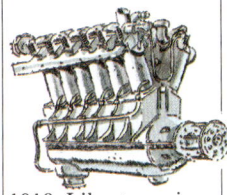

1918: Liberty engine, 400 hp, V-12 in-line engine

Section of a Liberty engine. Many of these American engines were made after the U.S.A. entered the First World War in 1917, and were used by the Allied air forces.

A sign of the times!
The mechanic is turning the propeller to start the engine.

The Flying Corps

The aeroplane began to be used for military purposes almost as soon as it was invented. The U.S. Army bought an aeroplane from the Wright brothers in 1908, France bought their first aircraft the next year and the armies of other countries soon followed suit.

This was the beginning of our modern air forces.

The stork was the emblem of one of France's most famous flying squadrons.

In Great Britain, an air battalion of the Royal Engineers had been founded in 1911, with one balloon and one

Some of the uniforms and flying-kits worn by airmen in the First World War

From left to right:
Belgian
French
French
British
American
German
German
American
Italian
British

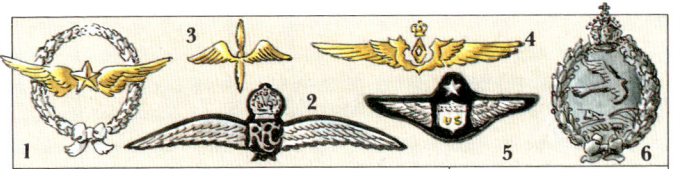

airplane. By the end of the year, the first flying-school had been set up. By the time war broke out in 1914, the Royal Flying Corps had been established, with pilots recruited from officers who had learned to fly at their own expense. It consisted of 179 aircraft and 1,244 officers and men, divided into a number of squadrons.

Air force insignia
1. French
2. British
3. Russian
4. Belgian
5. American
6. German

Aircraft markings
1. France
2. Britain, 1915 and 1918 (nocturnal)
3. U.S.A., 1917 and 1918
4. Imperial Russia, 1914 and 1916
5. Germany, 1915, 1916, and 1918 (two)
6. Belgium
7. Italy, 1915
8. Japan
9. Austro-Hungarian Empire, 1915

Aircraft at war

1915: a British BE-2C observation aircraft

Aviatik B-1, one of the earliest reconnaissance aircraft

1915: a Voisin LA-V, which was used for both reconnaissance and bombing. The row of lights under the fuselage was used on night-raids as well as for landing in darkness.

In 1914, the German chiefs of staff considered that an airman's job was to observe rather than to fight. Quite soon, however, aircraft were used for photographic reconnaissance, and then even directed the artillery from above: first using a signal code, then with lights and, from 1915 onwards, by radio.

An air-force base being set up. Once the squadron moved in, the site became more or less permanent, and hangars were built.

Many observation aircraft had their engines at the back, so that the observer could sit at the front, as if he were on a balcony, and have a clear view. These aeroplanes were very vulnerable; they had to fly low and could not travel fast, so they were within range of enemy anti-aircraft fire and could even be hit by bullets from hand-guns. What's more, their crews frequently got lost, and were liable to land in enemy territory to ask the way!

On 3 September 1914, Captain Bellenger in his Caudron G-III saw the advancing German army suddenly

PHOTO TSF

change direction. Observers were often first to spot major changes in enemy tactics. Special cameras were fitted on to reconnaissance aircraft; some even had a device which changed the photographic plate and reset the shutter automatically after each exposure. The pictures were developed in a mobile laboratory and sent out to every squadron.

The engine was so noisy that the pilot and the observer had to talk to each other through speaking-tubes.

Aerial combat

French pilot
Joseph Frantz
(1890–1979) went on
flying until he was 80.

On 26 August 1914,
Baron von Rosenthal
flew his Taube over
the Russian lines on
the Eastern Front.
An unarmed Russian
pilot, Captain Piotr
Nesterov, realising
there was no other
way to stop the
German,
courageously flew his
Morane-Saulnier
straight into the
enemy aircraft. Both
pilots died in the
wreckage of their
planes.

Early pilots went to war armed like
sportsmen, carrying pistols and rifles.
They were not supposed to engage in
any fighting, but the enemy crews
they passed returning to their bases
after a mission presented a tempting
target.

The first airmen to disobey orders
were Sergeant Joseph Frantz, a pilot,
and Corporal Louis Quenault, his
mechanic, who fixed a Hotchkiss light
machine-gun on the front of their
Voisin aircraft. As they flew over the
River Marne on 5 October 1914, they
spotted an Aviatik. They approached
it from above, in order to gain some
speed by diving down behind it, and
Quenault then fired 47 shots.

The German observer tried in vain
to damage the French aircraft with his
rifle. The Aviatik tipped over and
crashed in flames into a marsh. The
German pilot, Sergeant Schliechting,
aged 20, and his observer, Lieutenant
von Zangen, who was 24,
became the first casualties
of an air-battle.

The French aircraft
landed 300 m further on
in a stubble-field, and
local people rushed to
the scene with presents
for the victorious airmen.

Willy Coppens, in his
Baby Nieuport, used
primitive rockets
designed by Le Prieur
to shoot down
balloons.

Balloons

During the First World War, both sides used anchored balloons, as well as aircraft, for reconnaissance. These balloons were long sausage-shaped objects, with fins to prevent them from spinning round in the air. Unlike aircraft, they could stay aloft almost all the

1. Drachen
2. Caquot

time, so that each side could keep a continuous watch on the other.

There were, of course, attempts to burst enemy balloons with cannon-fire. Balloons were often punctured by shots fired from aircraft, despite the anti-aircraft guns which were supposed to protect them.

Anchored balloons were the favourite targets of the Belgian ace, Willy Coppens; he shot down 35 of them during the war.

An observation balloon back on the ground, being pulled along by its 'servants'.

The balloonist sent information down to the ground by telephone. His basket was equipped with an enormous camera, and was the perfect place for taking aerial views. Balloonists were the only First World War troops to have parachutes – so that they could jump if the balloon was shot down.

Léon Bourjade (1899–1924), the clergyman ace whose speciality was attacking balloons.

Nacelle

Airships

Germany, Britain, France and Italy all used airships from the very beginning of the War. Soldiers found them an unnerving sight – like huge grubs in the sky. But they were too easily damaged to be useful for fighting over land; anti-aircraft fire, aircraft, and even bad weather destroyed many of them. By 1916 they were being used only by the navies, for patrolling the sea.

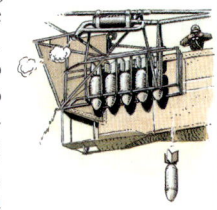

The Zeppelins which bombed London and Paris by night helped to give airships an awesome reputation. Huge machines, sometimes more than 200 m long, they lurked high above the clouds, safe from anti-aircraft fire. The bomb crews were lowered in a nacelle, at the end of a 1,000 m cable.

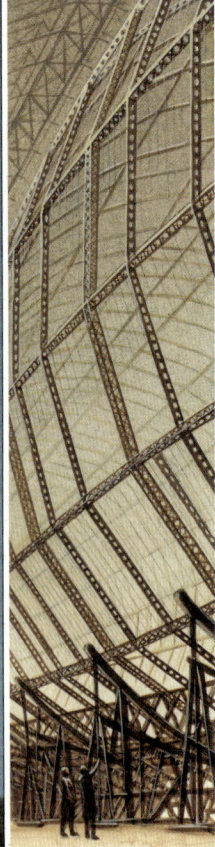

Airship frames were made from light-weight alloy, covered by a metal net and strong cloth.

Aircraft at sea

Ely taking off

Experiments by the American pilot Eugene Ely and the designer Glenn Curtiss resulted in the birth of the aircraft-carrier.

On 14 November 1910, Ely succeeded in taking off from the cruiser U.S.S. *Birmingham*, whose bows had been fitted with a wooden ramp. The next year, on 18 January, he landed his Curtiss on board the cruiser U.S.S. *Pennsylvania*.

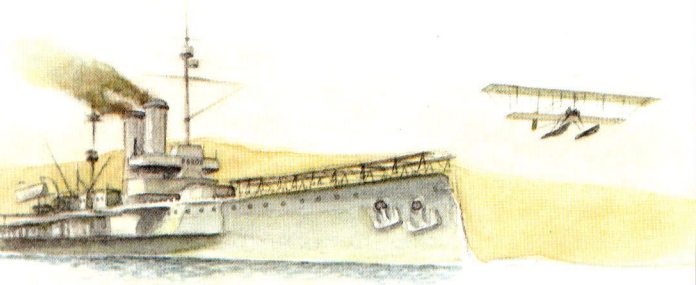

On 10 January 1912, Lieutenant Charles Samson took off in a Short S38 sea-plane from a ramp on the battleship H.M.S. *Africa*.

During the First World War sea-planes were used for reconnaissance as well as for dropping bombs and torpedoes. The German U-36 was the first submarine to be sunk by a torpedo from the air, on 20 May 1917.

Sea-planes were transported on specially adapted merchant-vessels. The first real aircraft-carrier was H.M.S. *Furious*, a converted cruiser which had a flight-deck 70 m long.

Two Short 184 sea-planes torpedo a ship.

A crane helping a Short 184 to take off

1916: H.M.S. *Engadine*, a sea-plane transporter

1917: the aircraft carrier H.M.S. *Furious*

The first man to land on a moving ship was Flying Officer Dunning; he brought down his plane on board H.M.S. *Furious* on 2 August 1917.

Aircraft-carriers played only a small part in the First World War, and no one at this stage realized how important they would later become.

A Sopwith Pup landing on board H.M.S. *Furious* in 1918. The aircraft was halted by ropes fixed across the deck.

The second successful landing of Dunning's Sopwith Pup on the *Furious*, in 1917. The crew rushed to grab the ropes hanging below the aircraft, in order to brake it. Dunning attempted a third landing, on 7 August 1917, but the aeroplane crashed into the sea and Dunning was drowned.

At first, shells were carried in the fuselage.

1914: steel darts (10-15 cm long)

1916: German Karbonit bomb (50 kg)

1918: the heaviest French bomb (500 kg)

At 6 o'clock one August morning in 1914, the people of Paris had a visitor: a Taube which dropped three small bombs. The same thing happened each morning for several days. A German pilot, Lt Ferdinand von Hiddessen, was making a determined effort to destroy French morale.

The Italians had been the first to attack an enemy from the air, when they fought the Ottoman Empire in Libya in 1911.

The British and French soon joined in. The French bombed the Zeppelin hangars in Metz in August 1914, using Voisins; a month later the British, flying Sopwith Tabloids, attacked the hangars at Düsseldorf.

1911: German anti-aircraft cannon

The first bombers dropped handfuls of darts, or even bricks, on the heads of the enemy. But soon the manufacture of bombs began. These weighed anything from 50 kg to one tonne, and were carried underneath the aircraft.

Larger aircraft were needed to carry these huge bombs. Some, like the Italian Caproni, the Russian Sikorsky and the German Gotha bombers,

Bombers

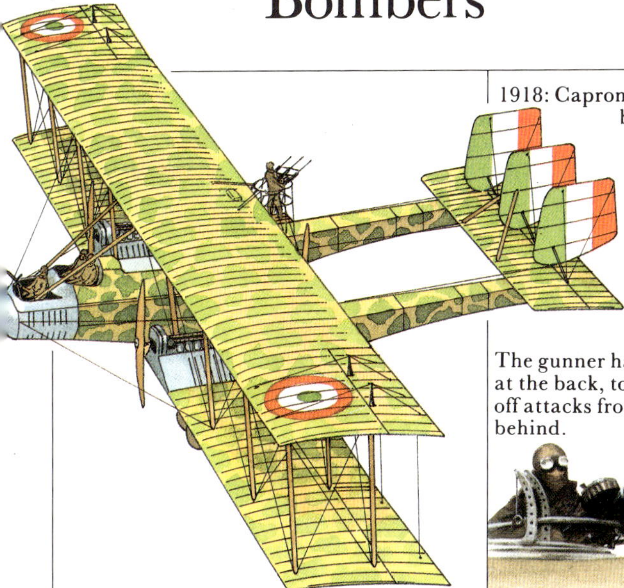

1918: Caproni CA46
bomber

The gunner had to sit
at the back, to ward
off attacks from
behind.

It is bitterly cold at
5,000 m, so he wore
special electrically
heated clothes, and a
leather mask to
protect his face.

were enormous. Largest of all were
the Zeppelin Staaken, built to bomb
Britain, and the British Handley-
Pages, destined to drop their bombs
on Germany.

People living in the cities were terrified as swarms of enemy planes roared
above them through the night sky.
The French even started constructing
a fake city on the outskirts of Paris, so
that its lights would deceive the
German pilots.

There were some brave but unsuc-
cessful attempts to stop the destruction. The Italian poet Gabriele
d'Annunzio flew over Vienna dropping leaflets which urged the
Austrians to make peace.

Handley-Page 0/400
with folding wings

Fighters

Lewis machine-gun on the front of a British FE-2B

Lewis machine-gun mounted on a Nieuport

Morane-Saulnier equipped with Garros's device

Fokker with synchronized firing

Fighters were fast-moving armed aircraft, designed to protect friendly observation aircraft and bombers, and to attack enemy planes.

As the war went on, aircraft design developed rapidly. Fighter planes became easier to manoeuvre and better armed, and soon they were a major factor in the war. Superiority in the air shifted from one side to the other several times between 1914 and 1918.

In the earliest fighters, the gunner simply held a rifle or a pistol. Later, a machine-gun was mounted on the aircraft, on a pivot at the front if the propeller was at the back, or else

Fokker E-I (Eindecker I), which in 1915 became the first plane to be fitted with Fokker's mechanism which synchron-ized the gun's firing-pattern with the rotation of the propeller.

1917: Morane-Saulnier AI umbrella-wing monoplane fighter

Checking the cartridges before they were loaded into the synchronized guns of a Spad

above the wing, high enough to avoid damaging the propeller at the front.

Early in 1915, Roland Garros invented a device which made it possible to fire between the blades of the propeller. Bullets were deflected from the propeller by a metal guard.

In April 1915 Garros was captured by the Germans, who found out about his device and ordered a Dutch engin-eer, Anthony Fokker, to build them one. Fokker's improved version syn-chronized the firing of the gun with the rotation of the propeller; the bullet could not be fired until the propeller had gone past.

Fighter design

The Spad XIII

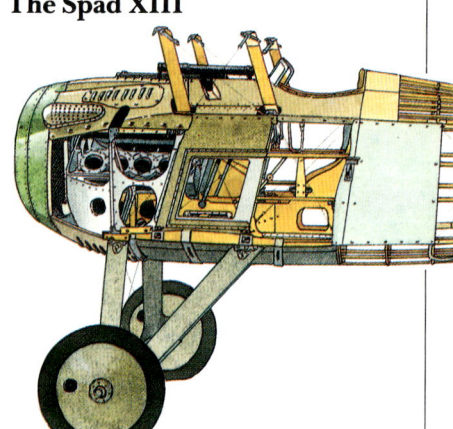

The controls of a Spad VII: the joystick (for height and banking) and the rudder-bar (for balance while turning and to correct drift).

A rear-view mirror on the upper wing of a Spad VII. These were standard equipment on First World War fighters, so that the pilot could watch out for enemy planes coming up behind him.

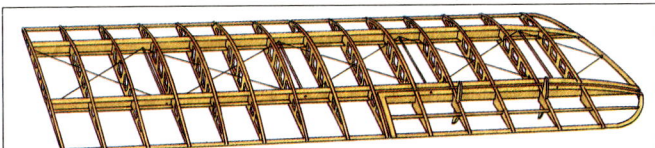

Till the 1920's **wings** had two long wooden spars, with ribs and wire struts.

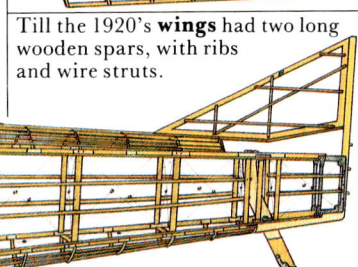

1917: Spad XIII
Engine: Hispano-Suiza V-8, 210 hp
Wingspan: 8.04 m
Length: 6.2 m
Height: 2.3 m
Surface area of wings: 20 m^2
Weight: 565 kg
Laden weight: 830 kg
Top speed: 205 kph
Maximum altitude: 6,900 m
Weaponry: 2 Vickers machine-guns

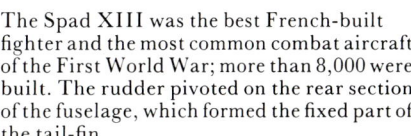

The Spad XIII was the best French-built fighter and the most common combat aircraft of the First World War; more than 8,000 were built. The rudder pivoted on the rear section of the fuselage, which formed the fixed part of the tail-fin.

Tail-fins and rudders

Aviatik B-II

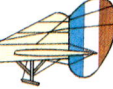

BE-2C

Nieuport XI

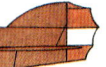

Phönix D-I

Siemens-Schuckert D-III

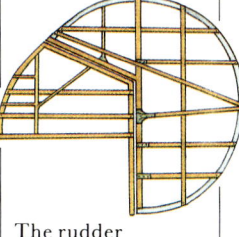

The rudder

1. Spad VII
2. Pfalz XII
3. Fokker D-VII
4. Nieuport XI
   (Baby Nieuport)
5. Junkers D-I
6. Morane-Saulnier
   A-I
7. Sopwith Pup
8. Fokker Dr.I
9. SE-5

The first battle
involving both air
and land forces took
place in 1918. Whole
squadrons came face
to face in the air.

Formation flying

By 1917 fighter squadrons had been established, with the precise aims of seeking out and destroying enemy aircraft as well as escorting and protecting slower bomber and reconnaissance planes. Combat developed from the early one-to-one tail-chases to dogfights involving 'circuses' of up to fifty aircraft. Squadrons learnt to fly in formation, practising flying together and avoiding each other's fire. It was at this time that many of the aerobatics manoeuvres, such as looping-the-loop, were first developed. The general public greatly admired the daring young pilots, who were seen as modern knights in shining armour.

9

8

Aces

Georges Guynemer (1894–1917) personified everything the French admired in their pilots. Brave, skilful and chivalrous, he destroyed 53 enemy aircraft, was wounded twice and shot down 7 times, before he was killed at the age of 23.

Baby Nieuport

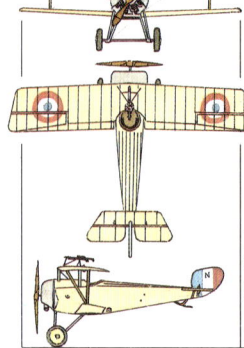

René Fonck (1894–1953), French

Ernst Udet (1896–1941), German

Edward Mannock (1887–1918), British

Edward Rickenbacker (1890–1973), American

William Bishop (1894–1956), Canadian

Francesco Baracca (1888–1918), Italian

Each of the aces had his own style; some were flamboyant and eccentric, others were calm and determined. The victories mounted up, but each evening there were more empty places at the squadron's supper-table …

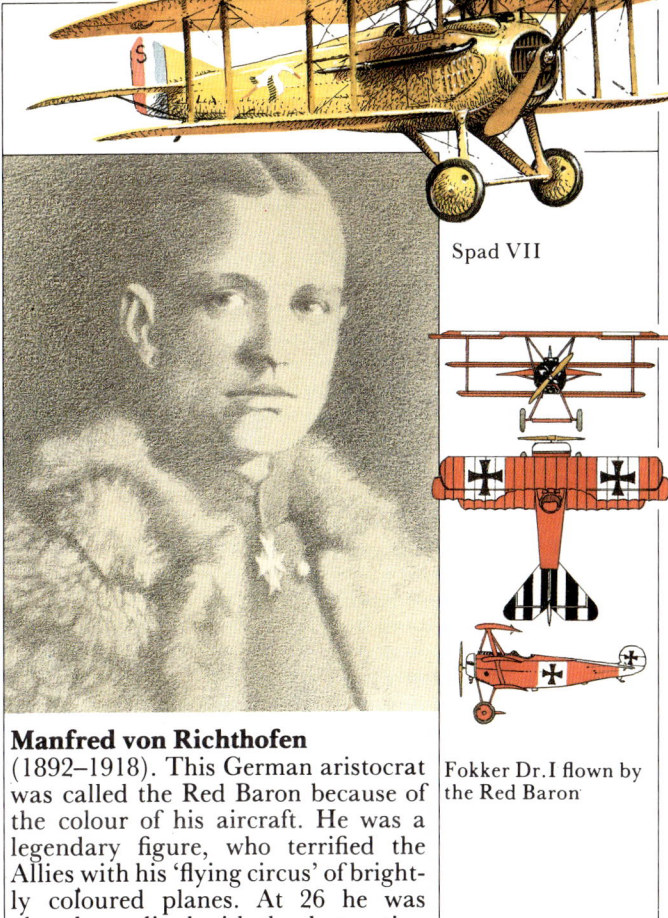

Spad VII

Fokker Dr.I flown by the Red Baron

Manfred von Richthofen

(1892–1918). This German aristocrat was called the Red Baron because of the colour of his aircraft. He was a legendary figure, who terrified the Allies with his 'flying circus' of brightly coloured planes. At 26 he was already credited with the destruction of eighty Allied aircraft, and he had an engraved silver cup for each one.

On 21 April 1918, the 'circus' was attacked by British fighters, supported by Australian ground artillery. In the skirmish, von Richthofen's aircraft crashed; his body was discovered later, with a bullet through the heart.

The aces and their victories

von Richthofen	80
Fonck	75
Mannock	73
Bishop	72
Udet	62
Guynemer	53

Mass production

Before the First World War, aircraft were made in small numbers by small firms. In August 1914, Britain had 84 military aircraft; France had 134; Belgium, 21; Russia, 190; Germany, 232; and Austria-Hungary, 72.

The war brought a great increase in demand, and firms had to expand rapidly. They took on many more workers: 380,000 in Britain, 190,000 in France, and 100,000 in Germany. Half of these were women.

Anthony Fokker (1890–1939), a Dutch engineer who worked in Germany, built his famous aircraft exclusively for the military during the war.

Brand-new aeroplanes waiting to be despatched to their squadrons.

Between 1914 and 1918, the British built 49,000 aircraft, the French 50,000 aircraft and 87,000 engines, and the Germans 38,000 aircraft and 41,000 engines. The average flight speed went up from 80 kph in 1914 to 200 kph in 1918, and maximum altitude increased from 1,000 m to 7,000 m.

On 11 November 1918, the trumpet sounded for the Armistice. By this time the death toll was immense; pilots, unlike balloonists, were rarely equipped with parachutes, and Britain lost 7,500 airmen, France 5,600 and Germany 11,400. So many deaths, after just fifteen years of aviation ...

A squadron worked as a team. Without the mechanics who kept the engines in tip-top condition, and patched the bullet-holes, the aces could never have flown.

The debris of war: surplus aircraft were left piled up in scrapyards.

Dare-devils

Aerobatics expert
in training!

Godefroy flew under
the Arc de Triomphe
on 7 August 1919.

When the Great War ended, tens of thousands of pilots were demobilized. Many of them had no skills other than flying.

Curtiss Jenny,
an American
aeroplane of
the 1920s.

Stunt-men performed acrobatics on aircraft wings, or hung by their teeth from a trapeze below. They could swing from one plane to another as they flew along, or climb into an aircraft in flight from a moving car or train. They even played tennis on the

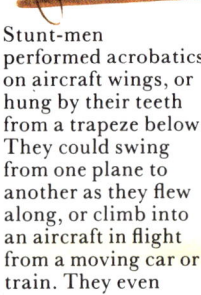

wings – though
without a ball!

A large number became stunt-flyers and travelled around, especially in America, giving spectacular displays at air-shows. Large crowds watched them spellbound, and there seemed no limit to popular demand. Hollywood also provided employment; pilots were needed to stage air-battles for war-films.

1919: Jules Védrines landing his Caudron G-III on the roof of a Paris department-store

1936: Marcel Doret in a Dewoitine D27

Aerobatic stunts were popular in Europe too during the 1930s. Pilots like the Frenchmen Doret and Détroyat, and the Germans Udet and Fieseler, could always be relied on to draw the crowds.

Clem Sohn, the American 'bird-man', at the Vincennes airshow. Like Franz Reichelt in 1912, he spread his wings ... and was killed.

Speed records

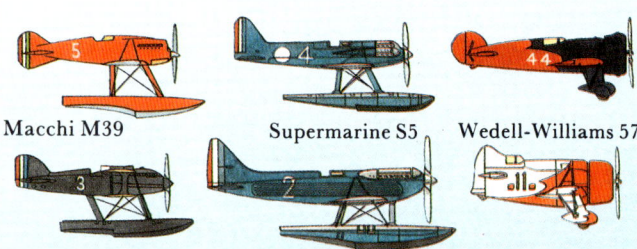

Macchi M39

Supermarine S5

Wedell-Williams 57

Curtiss R3C-2

Supermarine S6

Gee Bee R-I

Races
Louis Paulhan won the *Daily Mail* race from London to Manchester on 28 April 1910.

Claude Graham-White, flying a Blériot, won the first Gordon-Bennett Cup at Belmont Park, U.S.A., on 29 October 1910. He flew 20 laps of the course at an average speed of 98 kph.

Less than 3 years later, on 29 September 1913, Maurice Prévost in a Deperdussin won the Gordon-Bennett Cup at Reims with an average speed of 204 kph.

Between the two World Wars, various speed-trials, races and competitions encouraged serious research into aircraft design. Engines became lighter but more powerful; some could deliver 1 hp per 500 g weight. The most powerful (2,000 hp) had 24 cylinders.

With machines like these, records were constantly broken. In 1923, Sadi Lecointe set a new record for the eighth time when he reached a speed of 375 kph.

In 1928, Mario de Bernardi broke his fourth record with a speed of 510 kph in a sea-plane.

In 1935, Howard Hughes flew his H-1 Special at 567 kph.

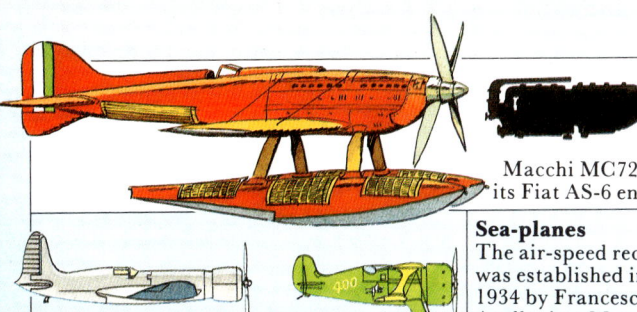

Macchi MC72 and
its Fiat AS-6 engine

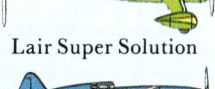

Hughes H-1   Lair Super Solution

Seversky Sev.S-2   Caudron C460

1933: Caudron-Régnier C366 built for the
Deutsch-de-la-Meurthe race

Sea-planes

The air-speed record
was established in
1934 by Francesco
Agello, in a Macchi
sea-plane which had
two propellers
rotating in opposite
directions to
eliminate torque.
He reached the
amazing speed of
709 kph; this is still
the record for a
piston-engined
sea-plane.

At this time, sea-
planes were much
faster than
conventional
aircraft. Because
they had an
unlimited surface
from which to take
off, they could
have short
wings, which
reduced
drag.

James Doolittle
1925: Schneider Cup
(Curtiss R3C-2,
average speed
374 kph)
1931: Bendix Trophy
(Laird Super
Solution, 358 kph)
1932: Thompson
Trophy
(Gee Bee R-1,
405 kph)

Roscoe Turner
1933: Bendix Trophy
(Wedell-Williams 57,
345 kph)
1934, 1938 and 1939:
Thompson Trophy
(Wedell-Williams 57,
399 kph; Laird
Turner R-14,
456 and
454 kph)

Jacqueline Cochran
1938: Bendix Trophy
(Seversky Sev.S-2,
399 kph). Louise
Thaden had been the
first woman to win it
in 1936.

Two famous air-
craft of the 1930s:
the Gee Bee R-1
No 11 (known as the
'Flying Death-Trap')
held the unenviable
record for the largest
number of accidents;
the Wedell-Williams
57 No 44 won a record
number of prizes.

The most famous speed competitions
were the Pulitzer Trophy (1920–25),
the Thompson Trophy (1930–49) and
the Bendix Trophy (1931–49). The
first two were flown round a circuit,
the third in a straight line. Most pres-
tigious of all was the Schneider Cup
(1913–31), also flown round a circuit,
but restricted to sea-planes.

Cups and Trophies

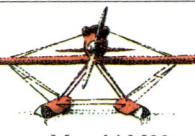

Macchi M39

The Schneider Cup

In 1913 Maurice Prévost won the first Schneider Cup in Monaco, flying a Deperdussin at 73 kph. This was an international race, and a country had to win three times in a row to keep the Cup. The British finally achieved this at Calshot in 1931, when John Boothman flew at 547 kph.

John Boothman and his Supermarine S6B, with a Rolls-Royce 2,350 hp engine

Sydney Webster, in a Supermarine S5, won the Schneider Cup at Venice in 1927 with a speed of 456 kphr.

Air transport

1928: a Fairchild 71
Canada in the far
north. The aircraft
was fitted with skis
for the winter and
floats for the summer.

Alaska, Australia, New Guinea, the Amazon Basin ... the most distant parts of the world became less remote with the arrival of air-transport. Some First World War aces worked as pilots and even as mechanics for the new small civil aviation companies being

1917: Avio 504. In Australia, the aeroplane took the place of camels introduced from Asia in the 19th century.

1926: Fokker Universal, with a closed cabin for 4 passengers; the pilot still sat outside.

1927: Junkers W34, made entirely of metal. This too had an open cockpit.

set up all over the world. Wartime aircraft were soon replaced by machines more suitable for this new purpose.

Flying once more became an adventure. Pilots flew into the wilds, carrying supplies of petrol and food. They surveyed land to be cleared for agriculture and building; they helped control fires and large herds of animals; and they flew back to the cities laden with metals from the mines, and furs from the trappers' camps.

In the far north, the engine was thawed by a stove under a big canvas cover—like an aeroplane's nose-bag!

Air mail

The first postal flight took place in India on 18 February 1911, between Allahabad and Naini Junction, a distance of 8 km. The pilot, Henri Pequet, was flying a Humber biplane.

The first international air-mail service (Vienna–Cracow–Lvov–Proskurov–Kiev) was set up on 11 March 1917, using Hansa-Brandenburg C-1s.

After 1918, mail was regularly carried by air. Many of the routes used were later taken over by passenger airlines.

Mail was first carried by air during the Siege of Paris in 1870. Nadar (1820–1910), who ran a ballooning business in the city, was put in charge of the operation.
He used 66 balloons to carry out mail – and people – usually under cover of darkness.
Altogether, 168 people and 10,670 kg of mail left the city. The balloons also took out 407 pigeons, which were then released to fly back into Paris with messages tied to their legs.

Man has become a bird.
And such a bird!
A bird which can think.
An eagle with a soul.

Victor Hugo

French Breguet XIV bomber, (1918), converted into a mail-plane for the Latécoère Company in 1919. Mail was carried in the two boxes under the wings.

In the early days of air mail, pilots found their way by following railway-lines!

Air postmen

1927: Laté 25

Between 1919 and 1930 airmail services were set up between France and Casablanca, Agadir, Dakar, Rio de Janeiro, Buenos Aires, Santiago and Lima.

On 25 August 1919 a regular airmail service was set up between London and Paris. By November, Aircraft Transport and Travel Ltd, which organized the service, had obtained contracts to carry mail from both the French and the British governments. The charge was 2s. 6d. an ounce on top of the usual postal charges, and letters handed in before eleven o'clock at certain London post-offices were delivered in Paris by four o'clock the same day!

The air-postmen had plenty of adventures as they flew over remote areas. Desert tribes captured or even killed any pilot unlucky enough to break down in their territory. The French pilot Marcel Reine had to

1930: Laté 28 in a zone of turbulence over the South Atlantic

raise a ransom of 4,500 francs for his release in 1925.

Even without hostile tribes, mechanical breakdown in remote spots was a perpetual danger. In 1929 Jean Mermoz made a forced landing 4,200 m up on a plateau in the Andes. He somehow managed to take off again, and virtually glided down into Chile.

Others were not so lucky. In June 1930 Guillaumet ran into a snowstorm in the Andes. He made a forced landing in a crater, but his Potez 25 overturned. He abandoned the plane and set off on foot; he was never seen again.

Jean Mermoz
(1901–1936)

1929: Potez 25
crossing the Andes

1932: Le Couzinet 70

The first passenger flights

On 23 March 1911, Louis Breguet carried 11 passengers for 5 km in his Breguet monoplane.

Louis Breguet (1880–1955)

On 17 August 1910, John Moisant flew across the Channel in his two-seater Blériot; sitting beside him was his mechanic, the very first air-passenger.

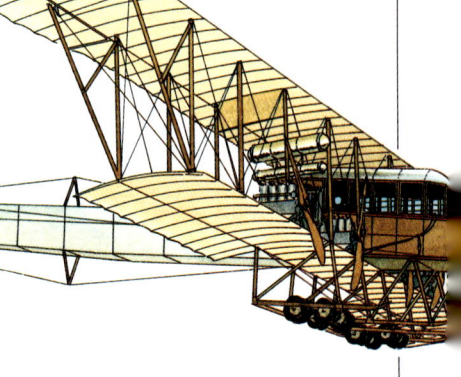

1913: The first four-engine aircraft, designed by Igor Sikorsky. It was later adapted to become the Ilya Mouriametz, the world's first luxury passenger-aircraft.

On 1 January 1914 the first scheduled flights began in a Benoist sea-plane, between St Petersburg and Tampa, in Florida.

Farman Goliath

F-AEGP

On 25 August 1919, Lt Bill Lawford took off from Hounslow Airport carrying one passenger, a package of newspapers, a supply of leather, several brace of grouse and some jars of Devonshire cream. It was the first scheduled passenger-flight from London to Paris. A single ticket cost twenty guineas and every day there was a flight each way. In the first month there were only three days of good flying weather, but the service was kept going and only two of the fifty-six flights were cancelled.

On the first airline flights the passengers sat on mailbags, but they were soon provided with wicker chairs, and port-holes for admiring the view. It was very cold; passengers had to wear an insulating paper 'lining', a flying-suit, gloves, and a helmet. A hot-water bottle was a useful piece of luggage, and so was an umbrella, in case of squalls. Air-pockets made everything in the aircraft shoot upwards, and quite often the engine failed, forcing the pilot to land in the middle of nowhere. Despite all these hazards, 2,019 passengers travelled between Paris and London in 10 months in 1920.

Popular passenger planes were Farman Goliath's, Caudron C25's and Junkers F13's.

Inside a Farman Goliath

Cloakroom of a Caudron C25

Junkers F13, the first aeroplane to be made entirely of metal. More than 300 were built between 1919 and 1932.

An Imperial Airways
Armstrong-
Whitworth Argosy
about to cross the
Thames as it flies
over London in 1926

*I am bound to confess that my
imagination supplied me at every
moment with the most realistic
anticipation of a crash... However, we
descended in due course with perfect
safety... Having been thoroughly bitten,
I continued to fly on every possible
occasion.*

Winston Churchill

The first airlines

In the early years of the airlines, pilots still had to sit outside the aircraft, crouched at the controls in the cockpit, at the mercy of wind and rain. Passengers, however, under cover in the cabins, travelled in increasing comfort.

In October 1919, the first 'lunchbasket' service from London to Brussels was started by Handley-Page Transport. Imperial Airways began to have two classes on flights between London and Paris in October 1927.

In 1931 came the Handley-Page HP 42, with soundproof compartments. At last, the pilots could exchange their goggles and leather jackets for gold-braided uniforms and caps.

European countries soon established air-routes to their colonies. India, Africa, the Middle East and Australia could all be reached – eventually, with numerous stops on the way – by large aircraft which could carry up to 38 passengers.

Hannibal, one of the eight Handley-Page HP 42/45s built in 1930–31 for Imperial Airways

The third engine

A Fokker F-VIIb, which could carry 8–10 passengers, at Croydon Airport

A Ford Trimotor carried 13–15 passengers.

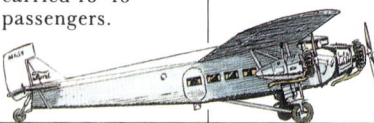

Between the two World Wars a new type of aeroplane was devised; it had one engine at the front of the fuselage, and one under each wing. The most famous were the Fokker F-VII (1924), the Ford Trimotor (1926) and the Junkers JU52 (1932).

The Fokker's high wings were made from plywood nailed over a wooden frame. It was chosen by several European airlines.

Junkers JU 52 (15–17 passengers) taking off from Berlin airport.

For their long-distance flights, the Americans preferred the Ford Tri-motor, which was nicknamed the 'Tin Goose' because it was made entirely of metal, just like the low-wing Junkers which never seemed to wear out.

Interior of a 1920s Ford aircraft

On 15 May 1930, on a Boeing 80 flight from San Francisco to Cheyenne, the very first air-hostess was employed to look after the travellers.

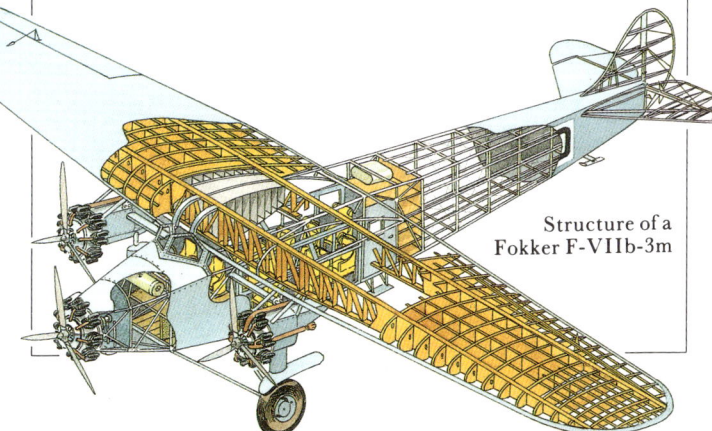

Structure of a Fokker F-VIIb-3m

Fly-by-night

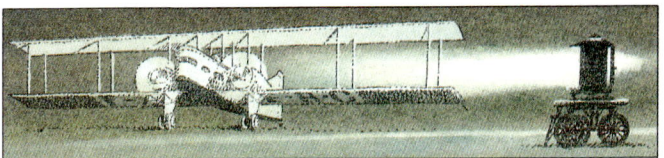

In the 1930s it became quite normal for air-passengers to travel by night. It was comfortable because the seats converted into couchettes, and now that navigational instruments were so much more accurate, flying in darkness was also safe.

Night-flying had been possible for many years, but the flights had remained isolated exploits. The first took place on 10 March 1910, when Emile Aubrun flew his Blériot through the darkness at Villalugano, in Argentina.

Henri Farman also flew by night at Châlons, in France. His biplane was lit by simple paper lanterns!

As early as 1910, attempts were made to provide markings which would be visible in both daylight and darkness. Both paint and small glass reflectors were tried, but quickly proved unsuitable.

In 1914 the Germans erected a network of lights on each of their aerodromes. These were either acetylene flares or electric lamps. Some were stationary, some revolved, some flashed – providing a whole code of signals to ensure that the aircraft landed in the right place. By 1924, airports in the U.S.A. were brightly lit and a system of radio-beacons was installed.

A Farman Goliath flew by night from London to Paris in June 1922.

The first night-time passenger service began on 1 May 1921, when a Junkers G24 flew between Berlin and Königsberg.

In the early days of air travel, runway lights were carried on a cart like this. They were put on the runway just before the aircraft was due, and tidied away afterwards.

Long-distance flights

4/9/22
James Doolittle flew a DH4B across the U.S.A. from Florida to California in a single day, with a stop in Texas on the way.

If commercial air-transport was to be safe and reliable, it was essential that the pilots, flying ever more sophisticated aircraft, should explore and open up new routes.

12/11–10/12/19
The first Australian flight home from Europe (Hounslow to Darwin) by the brothers Ross and

Keith Smith, in a Vickers Vimy.

4/2–20/3/20
Pierre van Ryneveld and Christopher Quintin Brand flew from England to South Africa in two Vickers Vimys and a DH9.

Alan Cobham

30/3–2/6/22
First crossing of the South Atlantic (Lisbon to Rio de Janeiro) by Coutinho and Cabral in a Fairey sea-plane.

2–3/5/25
First non-stop flight across America (Long Island to San Diego) by J.A. MacReady and O.G. Kelly in a Fokker T2.

20/4–7/11/25
Francesco de Pinedo and a mechanic flew a round trip, Rome Melbourne–Tokyo–Rome, in a Savoia S-16 sea-plane.

16/11/25–13/3/26
Alan Cobham and two crewmen flew from London to Cape Town and back in a DH 50J.

Cobham returning to London in 1926

Cobham later flew the same aircraft to Australia and back, again with two companions (30/6–1/10/26).

5/4–13/5/26
Callarza and Loriga flew a Breguet XIX from Madrid to Manila (17,050 km).

58

10/10/27–14/4/28
Dieudonné Costes and Joseph le Brix, in a Breguet XIX, flew the round trip Paris–San Francisco–Tokyo –Paris.

Jean Batten was the first woman to fly alone from England to New Zealand, in 11 days in October 1936.

Balbo's squadron

7–22/2/28
First solo flight from England to Australia (Croydon to Darwin): Bert Hinkler, in an Avio 581 Avian.

23/8–1/10/29
Chestakov and Bolotov flew an ANT IV from Moscow to New York via Irkutsk.

5–24/5/30
Amy Johnson was the first woman to fly alone from England to Australia. She flew a DH6 Gipsy Moth.

6/1/31 Italo Balbo and his squadron of 11 Savoia-Marchetti S55 sea-planes flew across the South Atlantic from Bolama to Natal.

28/7–26/8/31
The first flight from New York to Tokyo

1930: Amy Johnson's flight

via Alaska. Lindbergh and an assistant flew a Lockheed Sirius.

6–9/2/33
James Mollison flew solo across the South

Lindbergh's Lockheed

Atlantic from England to Brazil in a DH80 Puss Moth.

James Mollison and his wife, Amy Johnson

11–12/1/35
Amelia Earhart was the first woman to fly solo from Hawaii to the U.S.A. She flew a Lockheed Vega.

59

Non-stop across the Atlantic

8–31/5/19
Read's Curtiss NC-4

2–13/7/19
Round trip by the
British airship R-34

8/2–16/6/27
De Pinedo's Savoia-
Marchetti S55

1–19/7/33
Balbo's 24 Savoia-
Marchetti S55s

8/5/27
Nungesser and Coli
in the Levavasseur,
Oiseau blanc

20–21/5/27
Lindbergh's Ryan,
Spirit of St Louis

4/6/27
Chamberlain and
Levine in a Bellanca

29/6–1/7/27
Byrd's Fokker
F-VII, *America*,
which crashed at
Vers-sur-Mer
on a Paris–
New York trip
(5,600 km)

A prize of £10,000 was offered by the
Daily Mail in 1913 for the first non-
stop eastward flight across the Atlantic. In 1919, the millionaire Raymond
Orteig offered $25,000 for the first
non-stop flight from New York to
Paris.

Captain John Alcock and Lieutenant Arthur Whitten Brown won the
Daily Mail prize when they flew a

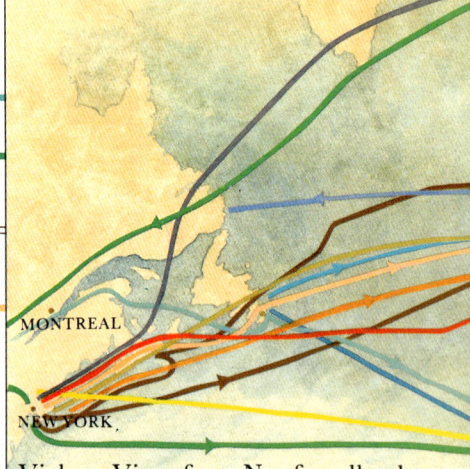

MONTREAL

NEW YORK

Vickers Vimy from Newfoundland to
Ireland on 14 June 1919; and Charles
Lindbergh carried off the Orteig Prize
on 21 May 1927.

The east-west crossing came later: the first non-stop flight was in April 1928, when Köhl, von Hünefeld and Fitzmaurice flew a Junkers W33 from Dublin to Labrador.

There were more than 40 attempted crossings between 1919 and 1933. Many of them ended in disaster.

REYKJAVIK

DUBLIN
BERLIN
LONDON
PARIS
ROME
BARCELONA
THE AZORES
LISBON

The first transatlantic flight was in May 1919, when Lieutenant-Commander Read and his crew flew a Curtiss NC4 sea-plane from Newfoundland to England, via the Azores and Lisbon.

14/6/19
Alcock and Brown in their Vickers Vimy

12–13/4/28
Köhl, von Hünefield and Fitzmaurice in their Junkers W33

13–14/6/29
Assolant, Lefèvre and Lotti in their Bernard 191

18–26/8/30
von Groneau's Dornier-Wall

1–2/9/30
Costes and Bellonte in their Breguet XIX Super Bidon

5–6/8/33 and 27–28/5/34 Round trip New York–Rayak (Syria)–Paris–New York, by Codos and Rossi in a Blériot 110

The lone eagle

On Friday, 20 May 1927, at 7.52 a.m., a Ryan called the *Spirit of St Louis* took off from the Roosevelt Field in New York. The pilot, **Charles Lindbergh,** was alone on board.

He had neither radio nor parachute, and all supplies had been sacrificed so that he could carry more fuel.

Extra fuel tanks between the nose and the wings blocked the view from the cockpit, so that Lindbergh had to use the side windows and a periscope to see where he was going.

To stave off hunger he had three bananas, some sandwiches, sugar, water and coffee. And to keep himself awake, he was sitting in a thoroughly uncomfortable wicker chair.

At 160 kph, the *Spirit of St Louis* set off into the unknown – and the unknown was not kind to her. The little aeroplane flew at various heights from 15 m to 3,000 m, lashed by rain, hail and snow, and buffeted by storms. High up, the air was freezing;

down below were the icy waves. After 20 hours of this torture, he was exhausted. 'I keep falling asleep with my eyes wide open. I know it's happening but I just can't help myself.' Eventually, however, **at 10.20 p.m. on Saturday, 21 May 1927,** Lindbergh reached Le Bourget, just outside Paris. Even the landing was difficult; the aeroplane bounced several times before all three wheels were safely on the ground. To his amazement a crowd of 100,000 was waiting to greet him. Souvenir-hunters rushed up to the aeroplane and started to tear pieces off it; soon nothing was left but the bare framework of the fuselage. Lindbergh, at 25, had flown 5,809 km in 33½ hours, and had become the most famous pilot of them all.

Paris – New York

The *Oiseau blanc*

The Atlantic crossed for the first time! Nungesser and Coli in New York at 10.50 p.m.! The French newspapers printed the story on 9 May 1927. The word had already spread, and in Paris there was wild excitement. But in New York there was no news.

The story of the *Oiseau blanc* is one of the most notorious pieces of false news in the history of the press. The aircraft never arrived.

What happened to it? No one has ever known, though there are all sorts of theories. The investigation has been reopened because debris which may have come from the aircraft has been found in a forest in Maine. If what was found does indeed prove to be part of the *Oiseau blanc*, the newspapers were right after all; the Atlantic had been conquered on 9 May, twelve days before Lindbergh's celebrated flight.

I will map out a path which in ten, twenty or thirty years will be used by thousands of aircraft and will become a major international route.

Charles Nungesser

Charles Nungesser and François Coli on board their Levavasseur PL-8 sea-plane, which they called the *Oiseau blanc*. The black emblem painted on the aircraft belonged to Nungesser, a hero of the First World War, who shot down 45 enemy aeroplanes.

All that remains of the *Oiseau blanc*: the undercarriage, left behind when the aircraft took off.

64

America gave Costes and Bellonte a heroes' welcome: a ticker-tape parade on Broadway.

The *Point d'interrogation*

This Breguet XIX was built for long-distance flights. It was christened ('question mark') by an exasperated journalist who was baffled by the elaborate preparations made by Dieudonné Costes and Maurice Bellonte before flying from Paris to New York.

Crossing the Atlantic from east to west is more difficult than flying from America to Europe, because of the prevailing westerly winds. Costes and Bellonte planned their journey with great care, and on 2 September 1930, 37 hours and 18 minutes after taking off, the *Point d'interrogation* landed at Cartiss Field, where Lindbergh was waiting to greet the crew.

The Poles

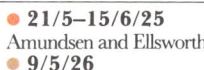

● **21/5–15/6/25**
Amundsen and Ellsworth
● **9/5/26**
Byrd and Bennett
● **11–15/5/26**
Nobile, Amundsen,
Ellsworth
● **15–16/4/28**
Wilkins and Eielsen
● **23–25/5/28**
Nobile

The North Pole

The first attempt to fly to the North Pole was made by Roald Amundsen and Lincoln Ellsworth, who took 4 crewmen in two Dornier-Wall seaplanes. They set off on 21 May 1925,

Roald Amundsen
(1872–1928)

The airship *Norge* made the first crossing of the Arctic ice-cap, and flew over the North Pole, on 12 May 1926. On board were Nobile, Amundsen and Ellsworth.

but returned defeated on 15 June.

Floyd Bennett and Richard Byrd were more successful; on 9 May 1926 they flew their Fokker F-VII over the Pole. Wilkins and Eielsen flew across the Arctic Ocean on 15–16 April 1928 in a Lockheed Vega.

Byrd also reached the other end of the earth; he became the first to fly over the South Pole when he piloted a

66

three-engined Ford Trimotor, with a crew of three, across the Antarctic on 28 and 29 November 1929.

In 1937 came the first attempt to fly from Europe to the U.S.A. over the North Pole – the shortest route. The first non-stop flight from Moscow to Portland was made by a Russian, Chkalov, who flew 8,300 km in 63 hours and 19 minutes. Another Russian pilot, Gromov, flew the direct

1925: Amundsen's Dornier-Wall flying over the ice-floes

route from Moscow to San Jacinto in California. Both men flew Tupolev ANT 25s.

On 2 July 1897 three Swedish balloonists, Andrée, Fraenkel and Strindberg, set off for the North Pole on board the *Ornen*. No trace of them was found until 1930, when the crew of a Norwegian ship found Andrée's body, his journal and some perfectly preserved photographic film.

Richard Evelyn Byrd (1888–1957)

1926: The three-engined Fokker F-VII flown by Byrd and Bennett

Uncharted territory

The Argentinian pilot Luis Candelaria, in a Morane-Saulnier, achieved the first crossing of the Andes at a height of 3,960 m on 13 April 1918.

Adrienne Bolland (1895–1975)

She was a French pilot who flew across the South American Cordillera in a canvas-covered Caudron G-III in 1921.

The American couple Martin and Osa Johnson used a camouflaged amphibious Sikorsky S39B on their African safari in 1933.

1933: the first flight over Everest (8,882 m), by Clydesdale and McIntyre in Westland PV-31s

Long-distance pilots became the new explorers, as they flew to every corner of the world.

In 1927 Francesco de Pinedo, in a Savoia-Marchetti S55 which he called the *Santa Maria* after Columbus' flagship, made a circuit of the Atlantic Ocean, including a flight over Amazonia right to the mouth of the Amazon.

In 1927–8 Alan Cobham flew a Short S5 sea-plane all round Africa, and made a film of his journey to show to the British public when he arrived home.

To the ends of the earth

The first flight round the world was made by an American army team. Between 19 March and 28 September 1924, their four Douglas World Cruisers flew 49,560 km in just over 371 hours.

As air exploration progressed and longer journeys became possible, there was still one feat left to achieve: a flight right round the world. Jules Verne wrote of going *Around the World in 80 Days*; Wiley Post managed it solo in less than 8. He took 7 days and 19 hours, from 15 to 22 July 1933, to make the 25,100 km journey on board his Lockheed Vega, *Winnie-Mae*.

The Lockheed Vega, *Winnie-Mae*, in which Wiley Post and Harold Gatty flew round the world in 8 days, 15 hours and 51 minutes between 23 June and 1 July 1931, two years before Post made his solo flight.

Between 31 May and 9 June 1928, the Australian pilot Charles Kingsford Smith and his three-man crew made the first flight across the Pacific, from the U.S.A. to Australia, during their voyage round the world in a Fokker F-VII B. They travelled 53,000 km between 31 May 1928 and 4 July 1930.

The Bellanca flown
by Pangborn and
Herndon

On 4–5 October 1931, at the end of their round-the-world trip in a Bellanca, Clyde Pangborn and Hugh Herndon made the first non-stop flight across the Pacific: 7,750 km in 41 hours and 13 minutes.

In 1938 the American millionaire Howard Hughes, with a crew of four flew round the Earth in less than four days (91 hours) in a Lockheed 14.

During this time of intensive exploration and rapid development, many aviators lost their lives. Death was a risk which they all had to accept.

Francesco de Pinedo
(1890–1933)

Jean Mermoz, one of the greatest pilots of the time, who had said, 'I want to die in a plane', disappeared in the Atlantic in 1936 along with the crew of his Latécoère 300.

In 1933 de Pinedo crashed as he tried to take off in his Bellanca.

Amelia Earhart and Fred Noonan, with their Lockheed Electra, disappeared over the Pacific in 1937. In the same year Sigismund Lenanevsky, with the crew of his ANT 4, disappeared in the Arctic. Saint-Exupery, who wrote *The Little Prince* and based his philosophy on his experiences as an airman, died on a reconnaissance mission in 1944.

Amelia Earhart
(1898–1937)

For these courageous aviators, flying was a passion to which nothing else could compare. Lindbergh spoke for them all when he said, after his solo transatlantic flight: 'I have been to eternity and back'.

Antoine
de Saint-Exupéry
(1900–1944)

An A to Z of Aircraft Facts

Ace
The title of 'ace' was awarded to a pilot who shot down at least 5 enemy aircraft. It was never recognised as an official title by any army, but in France and Germany the aces were heroes whose victories were made public.

Air-pocket
A downward current in the atmosphere, which makes the aircraft feel as if it is suddenly falling.

Altimeter
An instrument which tells a pilot how high he is flying.

Balbo
General Italo Balbo (1896–1940) became Air Minister in Italy. He was so successful at commanding formation flights that his name became synonymous with this kind of flying. He died when his aircraft was shot down by mistake ... by Italian anti-aircraft artillery.

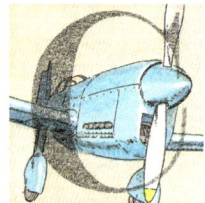

Cantilever
An aircraft wing is cantilevered: it is supported at only one end and has no cables fixing it in position.

Carrier
A warship with a very large flat surface (the flight-deck) where aircraft can take off and land. The first British carrier was H.M.S. *Argus*, built during the First World War.

Ceiling
The maximum altitude at which a particular aircraft type can fly.

Cockpit
The part of the aircraft where the pilot sits and from which he controls the aircraft.

Flying Corps
The name for the British air force during the First World War. Originally part of the Navy, it soon expanded and by 1918 the Royal Air Force had been set up with its own ministry. By the end of the war, the RAF had 22,647 aircraft and 291,000 men.

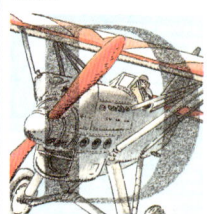

Duralumin
A very strong, light-weight alloy particularly suitable for aircraft construction.

Esnault-Pelterie
Robert Esnault-Pelterie (1881–1957) was a French scientist who first flew (in a glider) in 1903. In 1907 he built a revolutionary mono-plane, made entirely of metal. It had a rotary engine, ailerons, and an undercarriage which worked by oil-pressure. Just before the war, he turned his attention to the problem of space travel; he considered how to use rockets, how to travel to the moon, and how to fly round the earth at high speed. He wrote many books about his ideas and coined the word astronautics.

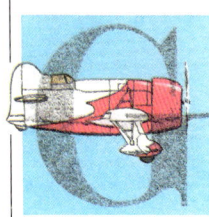

Garros
Roland Garros (1888–1918) was a Frenchman who escaped from a German prisoner-of-war camp disguised as a German officer, and rejoined his squadron. He was killed during a fight against a group of Fokkers when the engine of his Spad blew up.

Hangar
Shed on an airfield, where aeroplanes and their equipment are stored and repaired.

Immelmann
Max Immelmann (1890–1916) was a German ace who shot down 15 aircraft; he was known as the Eagle of Lille. An aerobatic manoeuvre is named after him as it was his favourite.

Imperial Airways
Set up in 1924, this was the first British government-subsidized airline to open routes to the Commonwealth. At this stage, aircraft still found even the Alps a formidable barrier, and had to refuel very often. It was quite an achievement then when the first route was opened, 1,800 km from Cairo to Basra (Iraq).

Junkers
Professor Hugo Junkers (1859–1935) became famous for the metal monoplanes, with cantilevered wings, which he designed. The best-known was the three-engined Junkers 52-3m which were first built in 1932.

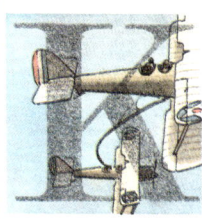

Kazabov
In 1915 the Russian ace, Alexander Kazabov, invented an original way of defeating the enemy: he dangled a balloon-anchor on a rope from his Morane, and used it to hook the wing off the enemy aircraft. He was later also credited with shooting down 17 aircraft.

Latécoère
Pierre-Georges Latécoère (1883–1943) started as a maker of railway-carriages, but later became interested in the problems of transporting mail by air. His company was responsible for a whole series of conventional aircraft and sea-planes designed for this purpose.

Lindbergh
In 1924 Charles Lindbergh (1902–74) was a pilot for the night air-mail service between St Louis and Chicago. After his famous exploit in 1927, he and his wife went on many flights into Asia and the far north.

Monoplane
When metal became the normal material for building aircraft, biplanes were replaced by single-winged machines, monoplanes. They were more efficient because airflow interference between adjacent wings was eliminated. At first, monoplane wings were supported by struts and cables, but later they were cantilevered. The wings could be attached to the fuselage at various points; at the bottom (low wing), halfway up (mid-wing), or at the top (high wing). Some were even raised on struts above the fuselage; these were known as umbrella wings. The Romanian Trojan Vuia, built the first monoplane in 1906. It didn't fly.

Nieuport
The French pioneers Edouard and Charles Nieuport died in 1911 and 1913, but their factory went on building their famous military aircraft. They concentrated particularly on sesquiplanes (biplanes on which the lower wing is smaller than the upper one). Their most famous model was the Nieuport XI, nicknamed the 'Baby Nieuport'.

Observation
The Italians, in 1911, were the first to use aircraft for observation and reconnaissance. During the war in Libya, Captain Piazza flew his Blériot over the Turkish lines near

Tripoli. Observation aircraft were vitally important in the First World War.

Orteig
Raymond Orteig was a French shepherd-boy who emigrated to the U.S.A. He became a millionaire, and founded the Orteig Prize in 1919.

Periscope
A tube containing angled mirrors to enable you to see round corners and other obstacles.

Pigeon
A carrier-pigeon will always fly home; the earliest 'airmail' service used pigeons with messages tied round one leg.

Plywood
Wood is weakest along its grain, and strongest across it. Plywood is made from sheets of wood, glued together so that the grain of each sheet runs at right-angles to the grain of the next sheet. This makes plywood stronger than ordinary wood.

Propeller blade
The part of the propeller which produces thrust and makes the aircraft move forward. A propeller can have any number of blades, but two is the most common number. In Britain it is commonly called an 'airscrew'.

Sikorsky
Igor Sikorsky (1889–1972), a Russian engineer, built the first four-engined aircraft, the *Bolshoi Baltiski* (1913). From this evolved the Ilya Muriametz, a big passenger aeroplane. Seventy-five of these machines were converted into bombers during the First World War.

Spirit of St Louis
This aircraft was built by Claude Ryan, of Ryan Airlines, in San Diego, California. It was first called the *N.Y.P.* (New York – Paris), but was later renamed as a token of gratitude to the bankers in St Louis

who agreed to finance Lindbergh's epic flight across the Atlantic in 1927.

Torpedo
A type of bomb which can explode under water. Torpedoes can be fired from a ship or dropped from an aeroplane.

Udet
The German ace Ernst Udet (1896–1941) set up his own aircraft factory after the war: the Udet Flugzeugbau. He also did stunt-flying. In 1936 he was put in charge of the technical development of German military aircraft, as the Luftwaffe began to arm itself seriously in preparation for the Second World War.

About the Author

After a hard battle with a group of three paintbrushes, a bottle of Indian ink, one tube of yellow acrylic paint and another of sky-blue, a formation of nine 2H leads, three HB leads, a squadron of blocks of water-colour, a sponge, and five sheets of blotting-paper (50 x 65 cm), the author, James Prunier, won a Golden Propeller at the eighth Méribel Festival for his first book on the history of aviation, *Pioneers of the Air*. The present volume is the second in a series of four titles he plans to write and illustrate to complete his History of Aviation.

Other titles in the *Discoverers* series: